Wanda—

Thank you for your support. I'm only blessed through blessing. You were a blessing today.

—Renee Collins

ALABASTER BOX

by

Renee Collins

PITTSBURGH, PENNSYLVANIA 15222

RoseDog Books
701 Smithfield Street
Pittsburgh, PA 15222
Visit our website at *www.rosedogbookstore.com*

ISBN: 978-1-4349-1206-0
eISBN: 978-1-4349-3915-9

I dedicate this work to the wings of my mother's prayers. Through her prayers, I've walked to, through, and beyond my life experiences to the safe place of inner peace.
This journey has taught me the true meaning of family, genuine friends, and unconditional love. Some individuals are in your life for a minute, a month, a year, or a lifetime.
The longer they stay, the more genuine their purpose.

Your Honor

When you are talked about, misjudged, the victim of malice, and envy, remember this—there is only *one* that can save your soul. Therefore, it is only *one* opinion that matters.

Me

The opinion of others is no indication that you are in need of
self-examination.
Be who you are, with God in the mist
Know that the others are on His list.

Sole Provider

The recipient of your daily meditation is the provider of all your needs. Thus, eliminating the value of judgemental statements made by those wanting to diminish your character.

Stand Tall

Stand tall, despite those who would do anything to replace you
Stand tall, despite those who would do anything to erase you
Stand tall, despite the hills and valleys
Stand tall, despite the stolen tallies
Stand tall, in the fact that you are saved
Stand tall, in the fact that for you, there is no grave

Seventh Heaven

The first I am, the first to fly
The second I am the second to die
The third I am, the third can't stay
The fourth I am, the fourth to go away
The fifth I am, the fifth to break
The sixth I am, the sixth he had to take
The seventh I am, the seventh to go home
God is forever in control
Therefore, my tears are now gone

The Light

Sun, moon, sky, sea
When you see light
You see me
Morning, noon, day, night
I am Savior
Thus, I am the light

Honey, Pass Me the Milk

Everyone knows that a bear loves honey.
At the risk of a taste, the sting of a bee could send him running.
As we chase material possessions, consider the one who created the
land of Milk and Honey.
To live there, only requires serenity to his will—no sting required.

Sorrow

From dusk to dawn, to a summer's end
A broken heart He will always mend

From Every Angle

Look to your left, right, front, and back.
Satan is always there, ready to attack.
But if there is prayer in the mist of this
action, he will have no satisfaction.

David and the Giant

Strength is the reflection of serenity to God.
For with Him every battle is won, even against all odds.

Gossip

Talk, talk, go ahead.... go
But it is your business you don't want anyone to know

Shoulder to Shoulder

Sister, friend you are the best
For it is we who stand alone when gone are the rest
So, regardless of the season, reason or hour, it is I, you can depend
on for your strong tower.

In-Law, In-Love

Let him go, let him go
For it is all of his business you need not know
For it is not I, but God that says so
Go ahead, relax, enjoy, your job is done
Before we were two, now we are one
Think of me as a day he went out to play
Instead of a friend he brought home to visit, I only came to stay
So when the grand kids come over to spend a day
You'll then realize, he never went away

Celebrate!

Celebrate, celebrate, and don't be dismayed
For it is an empty vessel the body has made
The content is gone far away to be free
Thus leaving no reason for tears from you or me
Why cry for the beloved to remain in pain,
When a place has been prepared for it to no longer sustain
Celebrate, celebrate, for they are free
Free to the bosom of the one that can also save you and me

Escape

A time to work, a time to play
A time to go nowhere to stay
Find comfort in knowing that when you're everywhere
You have nowhere to go to be there

Mistake-Resolution

Oh how easy it is to make a mistake
And often accountability we are slow to take
It's funny how quickly resolution we offer
When giving it to him first makes the journey so much softer
True, as humans, mistakes will always be
Just be sure to listen when he says the resolution is with me

Make Up Your Mind

Can I? Should I? Maybe at best
How will you know if you don't take the test?
First or last is not the task
So don't be ashamed and wear a mask
Placing last is an indication you've passed
For in your day, the first shall be last

Women of Color

Oh me, oh my, what do I see?
A berry called black, but sweet as can be
The outer shell causes such mystery
But make no mistake
Be mindful of her intentions before a taste you partake

To the Rescue

The birds in the sky, the fish in the sea
It is without I, they could not be
So have no doubt, I'd be there on the double
With the answer my child to all of your troubles

Blind Date

Late is my date, an hour has passed
But still I wait
For it is food that has not met my plate
So, sure I was that he had forgotten
It was corrected I stood
when the street said Peach instead of Cotton

Busy Bee

It's me.... it's me
Busy as a bee
Working on fulfilling all of your needs
So when the bills are due and
you are in the need of food on the table
Remember, it is not you but I who is able
Should a teardrop fall, make no mistake
With a tissue I will be there for I am never late

Aunt Tee's Baby

The sweet in my sugar
The brew in my tea
This who I call Aunt Tee's Baby
When it's tears that fall, in my deepest hour
She plays in the mist as if to see an April shower
When the smile she's used to is missing from my lips
She brings it back with just one hug and kiss
The heaviest burden seems light as a feather
For its you that make me laugh in any weather
The Lord up above knew you were too special to keep
So he sent you my way so that we could meet
Out of all the people I have come to greet
You by far just can't be beat!

A Flower in the Mist of Winter

A flower that never blooms is a symbol of unnourished potential
So sad is the day when rain is no longer needed

The Frog Who Became a Prince

The prince confused a potential soul mate
With a forbidden treasure box
A frog saw it for what it was worth and opened the box
A princess was inside

Surprise-Surprise

He came into my life offering escape from hurt and pain
Instead I was left out in the pouring rain
No flowers, cards, or cotton candy
Just someone who is found to be useful and handy

Life's Mission

My mission is to live, love, learn, and leave a legacy
Life is short, thus enhancing the importance to live
Love is forever, my love for family and friends will remain when I'm
gone. It's essential to learn all I can while I'm here. This will be the
foundation of the legacy I will leave behind

Terrorism

Who would have thought, with just a simple word,
lives could change forever, in any neighborhood
So loudly does the letter "T"
Represents the many tears shed by you and me
It is followed by an "E"
which demonstrates error that only anti-terrorists can see
The roar of such hate is the letter "R" ...triple take
So lonely the letter "O" that symbolizes the cycle that will never go
For "I" alone will not cause this to cease
For it is He that is above that will make it right yeah, you'll see
Yes the letter "S"
Just as sad as can be
But don't fear, soon will come peace eternally
Finally, "M" symbolizing the Messiah our dear friend,
for he will be with us always
Even until the very end

Time Heals all Wounds

My center focus—to heal, to define who I am and
to never compromise that again

Life is Purpose

If you made it here, you have a purpose
Regardless of the pain, the mistakes, the misfortune, the despair
You made it through every obstacle to fulfill your purpose
If you wake up from a trip through hell while carrying that thorn in
your side
You have a purpose
You were beautifully made
He perfected every living cell
He considered every part of you with care and precision
All to fulfill your life's purpose
So let yesterday stay with yesterday
For your purpose was not fulfilled there
But lives on through your next breath, your next heartbeat, your
next day

You Are

You are the ray of sunshine that warms my face in the morning
You are the reason I wake up early
You are the extra five minutes I take to do my hair
You are the future I was born to change
You are the reason I hate to see the day end because
You are here today, tomorrow you may not be
You are the seed that will grow our family tree
and your strength is why it will return every season
There's no "u" in "me,"
But without "u" there's no "us"